Any Ward, Any Hospital

Any Ward, Any Hospital

Practical and personal reflections

Roger Grainger

Illustrations by
David Bucktrout

 the bible reading fellowship

The Bible Reading Fellowship
Warwick House
25 Buckingham Palace Road
London SW1W 0PP

First published 1990
© BRF 1990

British Library Cataloguing in Publication Data
Grainger, Roger
    Any ward, any hospital.
    1. Hospitals. Patients. Christian life. Prayers –
    Devotional works
    I. Title
    242'.86
    ISBN 0-900164-85-9

Filmset by Eta Services (Typesetters) Ltd, Beccles, Suffolk
Printed in Great Britain by Bocardo Press Ltd, Didcot

Contents

For John Jackson

As we go around the hospital,
Go around with us, Lord –
See what we see
Do what we do
So that we may see it that much more clearly
And do it that much better.
For their sake and for yours, stay with us, Lord –
And when things get too heavy for us,
Give us a hand.

The Porters' Prayer

Preface

This is a book about people in hospital. I wrote it for patients, but members of staff may find it interesting too, as there's quite a bit about them in it as well. I had no particular hospital in mind – *any* ward, *any* hospital – nevertheless it contains all sorts of memories of being a patient as well as working as a chaplain.

It is divided into *thoughts, suggested readings from the Bible*, and *reflections*. The thoughts concern situations in the hospital, which I've tried to see from the point of view of the people concerned. The readings are passages in the Bible that fit the particular situation. These are taken from the New Testament and the Psalms, for use with the abridged Bibles provided by the Gideons for hospital bed-side cupboards. Don't be afraid to use these; things you may know quite well take on a richer, deeper meaning when you turn to them at times like this. The reflections are a kind of praying. They come between the descriptions and the readings.

The book is in three parts. The first consists of impressions of the hospital itself. The second concerns some of the people in it. This leads into Part III, which draws some conclusions. You don't have to read the whole book at once, however. I have tried to keep the sections quite short, in case you want to read something, but aren't feeling up to coping with very much. Similarly, they are all self-contained, so that you can dip into them wherever you want. You may find that some parts of the book mean more to you than others: if there is anything here to help you, the book will have served its purpose.

'Thy word is a lamp to my feet . . .' (Psalm 119: v. 105).

Part I

The Hospital

1. A place like this

A hospital like any other. Which means, of course, that it's unique. The important things that happen here, the things that speak so eloquently of the love of people and the care for their welfare are all unique. You can't mass-produce human sensitivity, nor can you mechanize whatever it is that is happening when real healing is taking place. The hospital is people, much more than it is buildings, machines, or techniques – which are only valuable in relation to the men and women who use them. And so it's people, always people.

If you asked the people who make up the staff in the hospital why it is that they work here rather than anywhere else, you would get various answers. As many answers as there are people, in fact. There's one thing you would keep hearing, all over the hospital, however: 'It's not just for the money.' It's something that is often overlooked, this deep love for the hospital. But it is a key factor in understanding the place, and the people who work here. In fact, it's what keeps it all going. Through all the hardships, difficulties and crises of the last few years – acute reorganizations, chronic threat of closure and redundancy – the hospital has survived because of the presence of a loving purpose, a deep personal commitment. It is a living organism because it is a *loving* organism. This is not to say that the spectacular scientific breakthroughs aren't important; of course they are. But so, too, are the 'little, nameless, unremembered acts Of kindness and of love'.

All kinds of people

People going on duty, people coming off duty.
Nurses, doctors, domestic staff.
All of them going about their business in a world they understand.
Here and there a drawn face and a hurried step.
This is a visitor, on his way to see a beloved relative.
Amid this crowd of work people he doesn't seem to fit.

They all know what they're doing, where they're going; he isn't sure, and stops, hesitating, to look again at the ward direction signs. One of the crowd going off duty spies him, and seeing the look on his face, goes over to speak to him. He smiles – an outsider, he is grateful for this insider's help. Look, he's off again, walking more determinedly now, as if he knows where he's going.

This group of people have brought one of the family into hospital. They are all talking as much as they can, to cover up the uneasiness they feel. You can tell which one is the patient because she hasn't said anything yet. The rest are carrying parcels. She has nothing in her hands.

All these people, going about their business, knowing where to go and what to do.

Except for the ones that don't.

Suggested reading:

Matthew, Ch. 10: 26–31 – 'There is nothing concealed that will not be disclosed, or hidden that will not be made known. What I tell you in the dark, speak in the daylight; what is whispered in your ear proclaim from the housetops. Do not be afraid of those who kill the body but cannot kill the soul. Rather be afraid of the one who can destroy both soul and body in hell.' The hospital's aim is to heal rather than harm – but there is much that is puzzling and frightening. This whole chapter is well worth reading for its description of people sent forth into unknown regions. You may not be feeling much like an apostle, but the part about sheep and wolves will probably strike a chord. Illness and disease are among the things that can kill bodies but not souls. Read *Psalm 34*, 'I sought the Lord, and he answered me; he delivered me from all my fears', so, 'let the afflicted hear and rejoice.' A real hymn of thankfulness in the midst of danger.

2. Coming in

Nobody ever gets used to coming into hospital. People who have been patients over and over again always say the same: you never get used to it. But then, you're never a patient really; it's the others who are patients, you're – well, you're who you always are. You're yourself. If you close your eyes and wish hard enough perhaps it will all go away; the pain first, and then the other patients, in that order.

If you think that this is a rather childish way of behaving, then you're right. But it's also a rather typical way. Psychologists tell us that the shock of coming into hospital tends to make even mature people react like babies. Having once given in and admitted that we're really ill, and need the special care that can only be provided in hospital, we tend to go the whole hog and relapse into a state of complete dependence. Over the years we have learned how to cope with all sorts of things, how to stand on our own feet, and to depend on as few people as possible. In this new situation none of this seems to work any more. The shock has been too great for us. Our carefully constructed defences crumble away and we are like babies again.

It's as well to be aware of what's happening, even though the truth may not be very palatable. Actually, this seems to be a very unpalatable truth indeed, and a lot of people are exceedingly loath to admit it about themselves. It's as if they're frightened of this as well – frightened of giving in, and frightened of wanting to give in.

Here's another cause of anxiety then. We're anxious because we're suddenly helpless, and can't admit it to ourselves. In our own way we're usually so sure of ourselves, sure of our ability to cope with things. But the hospital is teaching us something here, something about our need to admit our own weakness. As long as we refuse to face this we shall remain in the grip of an inner tension, and as long as we stay tense our real recovery will be delayed. And so will our spiritual maturity. It takes a mature Christian to recognize the truth about himself.

All these things . . .

Are you really sure you're all right, love? I mean,
Are your having enough to eat?

I hate to think of you having to do everything –
And the children –
Are you sure you're managing to get them off to school in time?
You know, I laugh when I picture you all in the mornings
All that panic going on and me well out of it!
I know I shouldn't but I do.
It was so nice to see the twins, love,
Yesterday – it really was, and I admit
They're both looking very well
Considering. Did you know that Sally's got
A hole in her sock, well, yes,
I thought you did, but I thought I'd better just mention it, just
In case. (You could have found Phil a clean jumper, too,
There's one in the airing cupboard.)

Did you get to the launderette on Sunday?
You know the one I mean, love? Yes, that one –
You knew it was open on Sundays, did you?
Yes, well it is. I'm glad I told you, so
You'll know next time won't you?
Mother rang the hospital last night –
Wanted to know how I was getting on: I said I thought
You were getting on fine! Don't forget
To ring her, will you love?
Tell her I'm coming out on Friday, with any luck, that is, and love –
You *are* getting on all right, aren't you?

Look after them for me please, Lord
You know how precious they are.
Keep them safe while I'm in here.
And there's this too, Lord – what I want to say is thank you
Thank you for them, Lord – I didn't realize, you see –
Maybe I'd forgotten, I seem to have so much to think about –
I didn't realize till now how much I love them

12

How much I really love them, Lord –
So keep them safe for me, I pray.

Suggested reading:

John, Ch. 16: 12–15 – 'I have much more to say to you, more than you can now bear. But when he, the Spirit of truth, comes, he will guide you into all truth. He will not speak on his own; he will speak only what he hears, and he will tell you what is yet to come. He will bring glory to me by taking what is mine and making it known to you. All that belongs to the Father is mine.' In the rest of this chapter, Jesus explains what this means in terms of human pain and joy: 'A woman giving birth to a child has pain because her time has come; but when her baby is born she forgets her anguish because of her joy that a child is born into the world'. Surely this must be one of the most encouraging chapters in the whole Bible. (Incidentally, Jesus reminds us of an important psychological truth, which is that in extreme situations joy and anguish tend to cancel each other out. People can't really be comforted until they don't need it! On this occasion, shortly before Jesus had to leave them in order to face his own death, the disciples certainly needed it . . .) Read also *Matthew, Ch. 6: 19–34*, a well-loved passage about anxiety. This is Jesus speaking, remember!

3. The team

There are, of course, plenty of staff, as well as patients and visitors. Every ward in a modern hospital has its own group of professionals, its 'therapeutic team'. This consists, basically, of the ward sister, the staff nurse, the house physician, the medical social worker, the physiotherapist, and perhaps a medical registrar. These are not listed here in any order of importance, because all contribute equally to the patients' welfare; nor are they in order of seniority, because they all belong to different hierarchies within the hospital: Sister and Staff to one, registrar and houseman to another, while the MSW and the physiotherapist are representatives of two more professional 'disciplines'. Again, Sister and Staff belong to one particular ward (or, perhaps, the ward belongs to them!), while the others may be concerned with a group of wards. However, as far as working on the ward goes, these distinctions do not, or should not, apply. On any ward, with regard to any particular patient on that ward, they all work together as a team.

Or at least they should do. But it isn't easy; in fact it's very difficult. It involves learning to understand and appreciate one another, despite differences of training and personality, by developing a common attitude towards the job in hand, a shared understanding of what is likely to be best for the individual sick person and for the hospital as a whole, so that this shared ideal is realized in the way the therapeutic team approaches each patient on the ward. Above all, it involves *time*.

In his image

Each of these people is extremely interesting:
This afternoon we have business with four of them –
Four graphs, four sets of notes, four lots of symptoms –
Brief verbal exchanges,
Short stereotypical conversations,

14

Looking and not looking,
Some questions, some comments, perhaps a demonstration,
All of it important, some of it vital.

So there isn't any time to talk even if you wanted to
And it isn't the right time, not during a ward round,
Just to talk to people, chatting idly, passing the time of day.
There is information to be gathered,
Instructions to be given,
No time for irrelevancies. All the same, it would be pleasant, my colleagues,
Yes, it would be very nice, my patients,
To sit by this bed and talk to Mrs Abrahams,
And listen to her news about her nephew Tom.
While the clinical cortège passes onwards round the ward.

Suggested reading:

Luke, Ch. 12. In these parables, Jesus teaches us about having the right kind of priorities in our lives. (A parable is a story about our own life in this world, told to make a point about the way God sees things.) In these parables we are given a picture of people who are determined to take every precaution to ensure their own advantage, as they see it, whether this be in terms of personal safety (vv. 4–12), material prosperity (vv. 13–21), or the necessities of life (vv. 22–30). Even the crowd are competing for the best places from which to hear him! Jesus says that not only do we cause ourselves unnecessary distress worrying about these things, but we don't pay attention to what really matters – our responsibility to the master in whose household we are fellow servants.

15

4. A chance to care

The kind of approach which is able to bind all these different kinds of people into an effective unity must be positive rather than negative. One which seeks to learn as much as possible about the sick person in order to be able to help him as fully as possible, rather than one which tries to limit the team's corporate responsibility to certain precise areas, certain aspects of the person's life which can be conveniently isolated from the rest of his personality and circumstances, and dealt with as quickly and efficiently, as antiseptically as possible. One which tries to embrace him as a person, not to deal with him as a problem.

This is the genuinely Christian attitude towards sick people. It is an attitude that increases because it inspires others. One or two people in a team who feel like this about their work will discover that before long they have influenced the work of the whole team. I believe that even one person can do this.

Warts and all

I don't know why they call them 'patients'.
I'm the one who has to be patient!
If old Mr Smith takes his arm out of that sling once more –
Look, he's trying to get it out again –
Lord, give me strength!
The trouble is, he won't try and settle down here –
He's not used to having people help him –
He won't let them help him!

Doctor was talking to him this morning
About when the time comes for him to go home again –
He wouldn't listen to Doctor, either –
Nor to the physiotherapist, nor to the social worker.
Staff's talking to him now: perhaps he'll listen to her.

16

She's got a way with him –
I hope so, anyway!
Perhaps I shouldn't worry about him – Sister on Ward 7 says it's not our job
Leave it to the 'physio' and the social worker she says:
They're trained for it, and paid for it, too!
But we're all in this together, Lord – Doctor and Staff, and me,
And physio, and Social Worker – all of us
All of us in it along with Mr Smith.

Thank you Lord, for letting us work together,
Even though at present we don't seem to be getting very far.
Bless, O Lord, all who work together here in a professional capacity.
Defend us from jealousy, from resentment of one another,
From the crippling fear of leaving ourselves undefended.
May love and concern for these your sick ones
Draw us together in a common unity of purpose,
A common desire to do all that we can
Both to know and help, and to be known and helped *ourselves*.

Suggested reading:

1 Corinthians, Ch. 12 – 'A body is not one single organ but many' (v. 14). This is one of the main ideas in the Christian faith, a really vivid way of expressing our shared life in Christ. St Paul repeats it several times in his letters. In this letter he adds to its impact by explaining how the body actually works, what its 'motive power' is. Read the next chapter!

5. Nurse!

Nurse!
Nurse when can I have a drink of tea?
Can I have a bed-pan, Nurse
Nurse, you said you'd change my dressing
                    – adjust this drip
                    – give me another pillow
Nurse, I can't sleep –
Nurse!
You haven't forgotten Mr Jones' bath, have you,
Nurse?
When are you going to get those backs rubbed
Nurse?
This must all be tidied away before Doctor comes round,
Come on now, Nurse!

The key to all this is the nurse her(or him)self, of course. These days nurses begin their training when they are eighteen – except for those in the orthopaedic section who can start at seventeen. Pre-nursing students enter the hospital at sixteen. So they are really very young to have so much responsibility; and the staff situation in most hospitals makes certain that right from the beginning of their training they do in fact carry a good deal of the weight of responsibility for looking after a ward on their own shoulders. In very many hospitals Sister finds that for quite long periods of time she has no trained nurses to call on, and could scarcely carry on at all if she could not rely on the help of her student. And when from time to time Sister is away from the ward, then the student is in sole command. She finds herself in a Florence Nightingale situation earlier than she had expected, and certainly much earlier than she would like; she doesn't feel ready yet for so much front-line responsibility.

But what can she do? The job has to be done, and she is the one who must set about doing it. Experienced or not, she is the person on the spot.

'On the spot' in more senses than one. As she rushes from bed to bed, trying to appear calm and efficient, she must wonder what she has let herself in for in choosing such a profession. It makes her angry that so much should be expected of her, and that now, when she needs support herself so much there should be no one to whom she can turn for help and advice. She feels she is too young to have to be so noble and self-sacrificing. Worst of all she feels guilty and ashamed to be feeling any of this. This is not how a nurse should feel at all. She feels she ought to be able to cope, with the patients and with herself, and she can't do so.

The others can, but she can't. They are proper nurses. She is a fraud.

And yet – cope she does. And completes her training, and eventually perhaps becomes a sister herself. She never forgets her 'baptism of fire' when she thought she was hopeless, a mistake, and found she wasn't. Necessity is a harsh master, but the lessons it teaches are thorough. To see these young nurses on the ward you would think they were much older than they are. It is not efficiency or a solemn manner that gives this impression, because even now they still forget bed-pans and they're always cracking jokes and teasing the patients. It is their air of conviction. When you listen to them in the canteen at lunch-time they are teenagers, adolescents, pop-fans. But on the wards they are *real nurses*. You can see it in their eyes.

Just a job

A pretty awful one, though, isn't it? I mean,
Apart from the long hours and the low pay,
And the sheer back-breaking hard labour,
Backwards and forwards, forwards and backwards;
You're surrounded by people worse off than yourself
So you can't really complain, can you?
But that's just it. You see
You want to help and you can't. Many's the time
I've stood here praying to God to show me what to do
To show me how I can help. Everyone else
So busy doing things, me just standing there

19

Uselessly, praying.
But that's not all. That's not all,
Thank God.
There's when you see things start to improve,
When time after time after time,
Sometimes just little signs, sometimes by huge great leaps
Huge great miracles
People begin to get better –
When someone suddenly turns to you and says thank you
And still you don't know what to do, don't know where to put your-
self . . .
It seems to me that this job is really about *not* knowing what to do.

Lord, you know what it is to accept responsibility,
Give us, we pray, along with your gifts of patience and courage,
the blessed gift of resilience,
The ability to live hopefully through changes,
And to face the future with eagerness.
Work upon our rigidly-held attitudes and opinions,
By the wonderful action of your Holy Spirit,
Which can transform bitterness into joy,
The joy of responding to new challenges and opportunities of service;
We ask this in the name of him who is among us as one who serves,
Our Lord Jesus Christ.

Suggested reading:

2 Corinthians, Ch. 4. St Paul is talking about the light of Christ, that
Christians have as 'treasure in jars of clay'. When you read this
chapter you will see what he means by this, and how it applies particularly to people who have a difficult job to do and a worthwhile
purpose to carry out. People who frequently get worn out.
Matthew, Ch. 11: 28–30 says the same kind of things, only this time
it is Jesus himself who is speaking to us – 'Come to me, all you who
are weary and burdened, and I will give you rest. Take my yoke
upon you and learn from me, for I am gentle and humble in heart,
and you will find rest for your souls. For my yoke is easy and my
burden is light.' Paul's life, as Apostle to an unbelieving world, was

very hard, and Jesus's, as Saviour of that world, even harder. For both of them the secret lay in the interchange of love. Jesus's burden is the load that is *shared*. (See *Galatians, Ch. 6, v. 2.*)

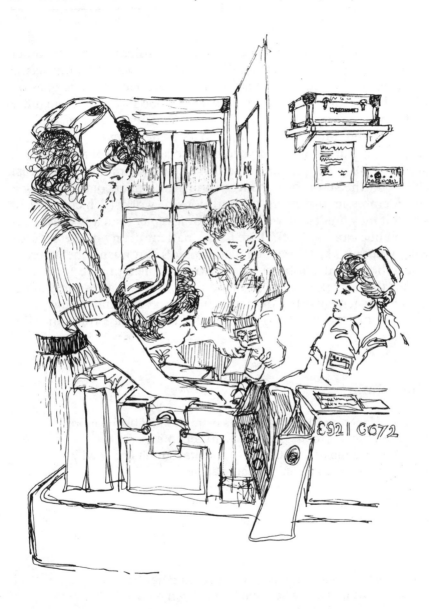

6. Angels

We do an ordinary job, they say, in an ordinary way. In other words we do our best. That's not to say that they aren't enthusiastic about what they do – enthusiastic and interested. As time goes on the technical and theoretical aspects of the job fascinate them more and more, and their training takes in a widening range of subjects which would previously have been considered way beyond the scope of a nurse's craft, psychology, sociology, group dynamics, dealing with grief and loss. The last twenty years has seen a vast change in the status of nursing as a profession, accompanied by a considerable improvement in conditions of work. (Which is not to say that they don't still work harder for less pay than any other profession one can think of. There isn't a patient in any of these wards who wouldn't like to see them better paid!) But it isn't the inherent fascination of the job, or its growing professional esteem that makes them work so hard at being nurses. These are simply additional inducements. It's the opportunity to care that brings them here. Simply the chance to care. And if that sounds romantic, I'm sorry.

Moonshine

There's a feeling of lightness in this ward. It must be the moon.
Everybody seems to be asleep now, except me.
And the poor old gent in the bed opposite, I don't know why,
He doesn't seem to be able to settle at all –
I think he keeps pulling his tube out.
Here's Nurse again, for the umpteenth time,
Backwards and forwards, forwards and backwards –
(She seems to be walking in a funny way, maybe it's her shoes
Or her feet) –

Lord, she's so good with him, so patient and gentle
Treats him as if he were her own father. I can tell you

22

I'd have lost patience with him a long time ago.
But not her. Not Nurse. It beats me, it really does.
There's a feeling of lightness in this ward.
Perhaps it's the moon.

Suggested reading:

John, Ch. 3: 1–21. God's gift of new life is not simply the old life patched up, although we tend to think of it like that, especially if we limit ourselves to what is reasonable, as Nicodemus does. Jesus reminds him of the way that Moses's staff was transformed into a deadly serpent before being taken up by him again in an entirely new form as the staff of powerful and saving care. So far as being human is concerned, there is no way round, only a way through, thanks to Christ. As the psalmist says, 'Even though I walk through the valley of the shadow of death, I will fear no evil, for you are with me; your rod and staff, they comfort me' (*Psalm 23*).

7. Doctor, doctor ...

First the nurses, then the doctors. Surprisingly, they seem even younger than the nurses. You can tell them by the white coats, unbuttoned, with a stethoscope hanging from the pocket, and the speed at which they hurry along, as if there weren't enough hours in the day, or minutes in an hour. And of course there aren't, not for hospital doctors like these. This must be one of the hardest jobs in the world. No other job demands so much, and is so badly paid, as this. Climbing out of bed for the third time to answer your 'bleep', after a particularly tiring day, must seem a hard price to pay for the eventual achievement of a degree of dignity as Senior Registrar. This is why the young man or woman who arrives at your bedside in the early hours of the morning seems so stiff and businesslike, so different from the genial Consultant you liked so much. This is why he, or she, isn't quite so tactful in answering your questions (if you dare ask any), but is even rather brusque. Who wouldn't be, if they hadn't slept in a proper bed for nearly thirty-six hours? Medical students and junior hospital doctors have to pick up skill in human relationships as they go along, learning more from their own mistakes than from lectures or text-books. There's enough technical stuff to learn, in all conscience!

No wonder they don't feel inclined to stop and chat. It's hard to be sociable when you feel like this. This is the time when the implications of the job you've taken on are most terrifying, and you simply put your head down and rush. One day there'll be time for the practised approach, the smile that calms fears and lends courage. One day, in twenty years, perhaps. In the meantime it's a case of getting on with the job, and trusting God.

On call

Lord, if I concentrate
Perhaps I can squeeze a prayer in on the way –

24

You see, I need to pray,
I really need
To pray. Lord, I've been thinking
(I'll just say this)
I've been thinking I may have made a mistake.
That idea I had, about combining
Service with Status
Turns out to be, in the event, somewhat
Impracticable.
It seems you have to choose between comfort and caring.
And now, perhaps, I'm at last beginning to
Get the point. Perhaps.
I suppose I should have known it all along.
Looking at you, Lord, I suppose I should have known –
Looking at you.

Here I am, Sister, I came as quick as I could . . .
Is he? Oh, that's good. What a relief for you! I think I'll just
Take a look at him.

Suggested reading:

There is a good deal on this subject in the Bible. You could say that
the entire Gospel is about the cost of caring, and our own involvement in this through our relationship with Jesus. 'Can you drink
the cup that I am to drink?' (*Matthew, Ch. 20, v. 22*). There is a
good deal on the subject in *Luke, Ch. 9*. There was nothing very
romantic about being one of Jesus's disciples, although, in the story
of the Transfiguration on the mountain three of them are given an
inspiring glimpse of the real meaning of their vocation, a vision of
the true identity of the person they were following. Jesus would
take up where the Old Testament leaders, Moses and Elijah, had
left off, so that God's triumph over evil would be complete. The vic-
tory is demonstrated in terms of healing in verses 38–43. Verses 51–
62 bring home the fact that it is not always so straightforward. At
least one disciple started off with a misguided idea of what serving
God really entails, expecting Jesus to be somewhat 'posher' than he
really was (*John, Ch. 1, vv. 43–51*). It is quite usual in this life to

'want your cake and your ha'penny'; sooner or later, though, you have to choose (*Matthew, Ch. 19, vv. 16–22*; see also *Ch. 6, v. 24*).

8. Not like you at all!

Being a visitor on a ward like this one seems to take almost as much skill as being a nurse, or shall we say that there are almost as many pitfalls involved in doing the job properly! Certainly you aren't responsible for the technical aspects of caring for the patient – but you have a particular responsibility for his or her state of mind. You have to remember that the person concerned has been lying there waiting for you to come and see them, a prey to all sorts of emotions, probably trying very hard to be brave, yet open to any kind of suggestion you might make simply because of the need to take all possibilities into account. It's an unfortunate fact that the more we defend ourselves the easier it is for people to slip under our defences and catch us on the raw. Attempts to 'cheer us up' often have quite the reverse effect. It can be a case of 'fools rush in' . . .

Not really myself

I'm sorry I'm feeling a bit down today.
You get bored you know, just lying here.
No, I don't know how long I shall be like this.
I'm sorry, I'm feeling a bit down today.

I really don't know how I can carry on –
It seems to go on for ever.
I think it'll outlast me . . . I really do.
I was in that bed, the one that turns from side to side,
The one that turns from
Side to side, so as not to put too much
Pressure on my wound,
For two and a half months, or more –
I sat out of bed just six times, and it broke out again
I think it'll outlast me.
And so here I am,

27

Back again where I started from.
Again.
Is it ever going to be finished?

I'm sorry, I'm feeling a bit down today.
Perhaps I'll feel better. Anyway –
Thanks for the prayer. You know, I do
Appreciate it.

Suggested reading:

John, Ch. 9: 1–7. Someone else's pain has a powerful effect on the
people around. Remember Job and his comforters! In this passage
the disciples are thrown into confusion by their need to reconcile
their natural feelings of compassion with the demands of their call-
ing as disciples of Jesus, and therefore specialists in right and
wrong. They ask for a theological judgement from Jesus: let him
decide whose fault it is. Where they see faults, he sees opportunities,
ways of revealing the extent and power of God's love. Whatever
happens, God's love will somehow be revealed to men and women.
Love is paramount; we should not dwell on what appears to us to
be evidence of divine anger, but learn to see signs of love. In *1 Peter,
Ch. 3: v. 8*, we read, 'Finally, all of you, live in harmony with one
another; be sympathetic, love as brothers, be compassionate and
humble', while St Paul, in *Romans, Ch. 15: v. 1*, tells us that 'we who
are strong ought to bear with the failings of the weak'. I can't help
feeling that he is using a little gentle irony here. Certainly he knew
all about feeling weak himself! This chapter overflows with joy, and
should be read often – 'may you overflow with hope'.

9. Joy

Perhaps there's something here which may help us when we visit fellow members of our congregation who are in hospital. Christian joy is the greatest gift you can bring to anybody who is sick, because Christian joy is resurrection-joy; it is a new life, new hope, in the presence of despair, even of death itself. As such it has the power to lighten the heaviest load of suffering. This is a fact; and it has been demonstrated over and over again.

But it is also a fact that there is a great deal of difference between talking about, or singing about, Christian joy, and actually communicating it. This is why so much of the effort put in by individuals and groups of people in doing their Christian duty with regard to the sick has precisely the opposite effect from the one intended, so that patients who are the objects of all this attention are alienated rather than consoled, because they see the whole enterprise as an attempt to take advantage of their dependent position in order to get at them and make them feel guilty for not going to church, or not reading their Bibles, or whatever. Which is bad enough in itself – but to do this and talk about joy at the same time is really going too far! That is really adding insult to injury!

To communicate Christian joy you have to experience it; and not in theory, but in fact. By which I mean you have to be experiencing it at the time. If this is what is happening to you, then you have no problems at all. Your joy will share itself. You will share yourself. Your singing and praying and talking will no longer be *at* people, but *with* them. After all, people are surprisingly willing to take things in the spirit in which they're offered. Particularly sick people.

And, of course, there are other ways of communicating love, apart from the verbal way. People use the language of touch a lot in hospitals. Much of what is said is unintentional: consider for example, the way that the houseman gives an injection – 'I can do this as efficiently as Sister, there's nothing to it.' (When Sister does it, you hardly notice it at all!) A good deal is impersonal, as it must be in emergencies. Even so, it is surprising how eloquently these functional tasks are performed: how much kindness in the way the blanket is tucked in around this lady who is setting off on the journey to the Operating Theatre, how carefully the Domestic rearranges the precious photographs on top of the locker. People who don't usually hold hands with strangers, find themselves doing quite a lot of that sort of thing in hospital. There's so much to be said, you see, and you find yourself strangely unable to say it. Even if you can find the words, they can be very hard to get out. Which is why you tend to use the language of touch instead. It isn't that you make a conscious decision – you just find yourself reaching out to someone. Everybody does it, not just people who are new to the place. The professionals here are always coming across situations which lie beyond the reach of words. Reaching out and touching can be a valuable part of hospital expertise.

Gently does it . . .

My hand is heavy in this frail wrist
I ease its weight, trying not to press so hard.
And as I lift my fingers the hand comes up to meet me.
Don't stop, it says, stay where you are a minute longer . . .
I don't want to go, I don't want to take my hand away.
And use it for all those other things I make it do.
All those necessary, important things I make it do.
Just for the moment my hand is happy where it is
And I'll leave it be. My fingers are comforted by this venerable skin
Shiny, translucent, like old parchment,
A life-time written on it. What's the rush it says
Where are you going that's so important,
What's this job that just can't wait? Stay a moment,
Don't be rushing off, Stay here with me
While there's still time. I won't press you (I'm hardly touching you)
What's another five minutes . . . Eloquent wrist, arguing so persuasively
While your owner is fast asleep.

Suggested reading:

John, Ch. 13: 1–15 – 'If I then, your Lord and Master, have washed your feet, ye also ought to wash one another's feet.' Sharing again, sharing and caring. This washing is not to cleanse from sin, as in Baptism. Jesus makes this clear to Peter. This is to comfort and refresh, and thereby to show love. In a way it is *like* a sacrament, being the 'outward and physical sign of an inward and spiritual grace', but the grace concerned is simple, ordinary loving, albeit on the part of the Son of God. You could call it the sacrament of 'little, nameless, unremembered acts Of kindness and of love'. There are many examples in the Bible of people touching each other to heal and comfort. The line between healing and comforting is by no means a hard and fast one, as a gentle touch may soothe pain away by quietening our nervous system.

10. There's no time now

Not any time. Not much encouragement either. There's always a job to be done. People who do counselling work of any kind – marriage-guidance counsellors, Samaritans, hospital chaplains, counsellors in schools – are always very much aware of the dangers of 'getting involved'. To get involved is to get *too* involved, to become so taken up into someone's 'problem', the emotional, inter-personal difficulty that is causing them distress, getting in the way of their work and making relaxation of any kind impossible for them, that you inherit the very condition you are trying to relieve. You start out trying to help, and end up in a worse state than the person who has come to you for help.

Well, this is the story anyway. That is what people say. In certain circles it even goes without saying. Traditionally, it has been taught in general nursing schools that too much concern for a patient's state of mind, too much awareness of the details of his or her pri-vate life, is likely to interfere with nursing efficiency. Nurses, like doctors, adopt a 'bedside manner' in order to prevent themselves being drawn into things which are no concern of theirs, and are liable to distract them from the business of healing people.

It isn't true of course. The truth, in fact, is quite the opposite. Healing takes place where sick people are accepted as themselves. You can't simply isolate the part of a sick man or woman that you are able to cure from all the rest of his personality, and get to work on that, as if you were an atomic scientist dealing with isotopes behind radiation-proof glass. It is personal involvement that actually heals people; refusal to be involved can actually cause a lot of harm, because it confirms sick people in their alienation, their feeling of not belonging, not being worth caring about. If someone reveals their need to you and you remain completely detached, you are like a surgeon, who, having made his incision, simply gazes on the wound and leaves it at that. Indeed it is worse than this, because it offends the distressed person in the very place where he sustained his original injury – his sense of personal worth.

So you've got to be willing to get involved. You've got to be willing to suffer too. Perhaps this may mean going through a phase in the relationship when you really don't seem to be being much help, because you are too distressed to be very practical. One might even say that it is necessary for you to go through this stage. It is the pledge of the reality of your concern for the person who has asked for your help. It is something that you go through together, which because it is a genuine shared experience has a way of changing things.

Time to be practical and professional afterwards. It might even work, then.

Watch your step

Sister says don't ever
Get involved.
We try on this ward
To give as much time to each patient
As to all the rest. We don't
Have favourites.
Sister says it's not fair
I'm sure she's right. In the corner there's Stephen.
He's very brave and not very old.
My heart goes out to him. So does Sister's
But she's tough and doesn't show it.
It's the same with all of them: Mr Williams,
Mrs Frobisher, Mr Andrews.
All the same, all patients, all to be cared for in the
Same way. Don't
Get involved.

I'm sure she's right. One thing, though –
She doesn't practise what she preaches.
Or so it seems. She told me yesterday she'd been talking
To Mr Andrews about the folks at home, his family.
Do you know, she said, it could be mine?
I didn't say a word because she's right.
It is hers, isn't it? She's wiser than she thinks,
Sister. For how can you begin to help

Unless you understand? And if you want to understand
You've got to share.

Suggested reading:

John, Ch. 1: 1–18. John the Baptist witnesses to the fact that Jesus is the Word become flesh – in other words that he is the active power of God and his presence among men and women to save them: 'the law was given through Moses; grace and truth came through Jesus Christ'. This marvellous chapter needs a certain amount of concentration if you want to try and get the best out of it. However, the words are so lovely that you'll receive great comfort by just reading them through as if it were a poem (which it is!). In *Ch. 3: v. 16* Jesus says 'For God so loved the world that he gave his only begotten Son, that whoever believes in him shall not perish but have eternal life'. The whole Gospel of St John is about *involvement*; God's involvement with his world comes home to us more powerfully here than anywhere else. We have a whole new deal, of course we must have a new birth! Nicodemus cannot grasp the extent of God's revolution, which goes beyond being described in literal language.

11. Where the buck stops

Once you understand, you have to make choices about what to *do*. In hospital this is particularly difficult. Everybody admires people who have strong principles. But what does having principles mean? What is a principle? Is it the same as an inflexible rule? A man who always obeys the same rules in whatever circumstances may be admired for consistency; it would be difficult to commend him always for courage, because there will be some occasion surely, when his rule-following behaviour will provide him with a most thankfully convenient way of evading what he knows to be his true responsibility. Unless, of course, he feels that his responsibility is simply and solely to be a rule-follower.

Rules are always misleading anyway. Does the rule 'Thou shalt not kill' mean, in effect, that 'thou shalt devise ways in which people may take the longest possible time dying'? Does the Christian understanding about the sacredness of life refer to quantity rather than quality; must life be preserved whatever the quality, whatever the cost?

The tendency in hospital is to see death in terms of defeat. This is not the way Christian people are to regard dying. Not to be able to contemplate death, not to be able, in certain circumstances, to allow people to die, is itself a worse kind of defeat than physical death, the death of the organism, could ever be. This, for Christians – and indeed for all who claim that there is meaning in life which transcends mere length of days – is a death of the soul.

But this attitude to life and death demands maturity. The doctor who can allow himself to follow the law of love rather than slavishly obeying a fixed rule of fear must always, must necessarily, be involved in making decisions. These decisions will concern not only him, but everyone in the ward. Whatever the doctor and Sister decide to do about Mr Thompson, it is to be hoped that Sister will take the student nurse into her confidence about it. Even if responsibility cannot be shared, the reasons for decisions taken can and should be understood.

Decisions

I suppose you could say that there are two schools of thought
(I wonder how they'll take this?)
Two schools.
At this hospital, unless we are reasonably sure of a successful outcome,
We don't perform the operation.
At another hospital – not fifty miles away from this one –
Whatever the prognosis, the surgeons always operate.
You think so? Well, I'm not surprised . . .
(Oh Lord, why is it they never seem to understand?)
However,
I personally do not care to sentence another human being, someone like myself
To a lifetime of humiliating dependence and frequent uncontrollable pain.
But I have no doubt that on this issue
Some of you here will disagree with me, perhaps quite violently.
So at the end of my talk we will go into the ward
And look at some cases.
(And then perhaps some of you will be persuaded to change your minds!)
Oh yes, I understand that, and, of course, in principle I agree –
In principle but not *on* principle . . .

How I envy them, Lord,
The people who know they are right,
Those for whom matters of life and death are a matter of procedure,
Simply a matter of sticking closely to the rules,
People who are able to make every decision according to the book,
Who don't make any real decisions at all.
But the fact is, that when I come to read it,
Yours is a very puzzling book, Lord.

Suggested reading:

Psalm 32. The psalmist has taken his confusion to God. As a result he knows he is forgiven. In verse 8, God tells him that he will always receive guidance, so long as he is humble enough to ask for it, and not so stubborn that he refuses to take it. In *Psalm 119: 105–112*, the psalmist thanks God for the help he receives from reading the scriptures. 'Your word is a lamp to my feet and a light for my path'. For the finest example of someone asking God for guidance, read the passage in St Mark's Gospel where Jesus prays to his Father in the Garden of Gethsemane, before he is captured and taken away to be crucified (*Mark, Ch. 14: 32–41*). In this case, of course, Jesus knows what he must do. He asks for the ability to do it.

12. Investigation

And, of course, the uncertainty isn't confined to the staff. As usual it's the patients who suffer most. Take coming into hospital for investigation, for instance. In some ways, this is the worst thing of all; worse than coming in for a definite operation. It can be extremely uncomfortable of course, because some of the tests that are carried out can be painful, and even being X-rayed, when you are feeling ill, is a considerable strain. These are the facts of life at present, anyhow. Perhaps, as medical knowledge advances, someone may find a way of making investigatory procedures less exhausting to the patient.

But the worst thing about the situation is not the physical discomfort but the psychological strain. 'If only they'd find out what's wrong with me and get on with it. I wouldn't mind what it was, if only I knew what I was in for. I can't stand all this waiting around. I've been here a fortnight now and all I've had is tests.' Patients get bored and frustrated and often attempt – sometimes successfully – to discharge themselves from hospital before anything has really been attempted in the way of actual therapy.

But of course you can't begin treatment until you've arrived at an adequate diagnosis. This fact seems obvious enough. Why is it then, that quite intelligent and mature people seem unable to accept it? I think there are two reasons, the second following on from the first. The first is a growing belief in the omniscience of medical science. Patients find it harder and harder to accept the suggestion that the doctors may not know what is wrong with them. A few may boast rather feebly about baffling everybody with a rare condition, but most simply don't believe that there's any real problem about finding out what the matter is. Not nowadays; not with all this new machinery. And what about that article I read in Reader's Digest last month, about a case just like mine? And if the doctor really does know what's the matter, but isn't going to say – in other words, he's pretending ignorance of the facts which are really at his finger-tips – then there's only one conclusion to be drawn. The facts are too serious to be told. They're not telling me in order to protect me. And if that's the case, I'd rather be at home, in my own bed!

All this may seem absurd. It is absurd. Nevertheless, it is the way the mind seems to work under stress. And there's nothing like the uncertainty and tension of waiting about in hospital, in the presence of people who are demonstrably ill, to start you thinking about these things. People who feel like this, who are going through this phase, don't get much sympathy. Nobody knows what to be sympathetic *about*. People find it much easier to show concern for identifiable physical conditions than for vague psychological states. Yet it is an awful state of mind to be in, and certainly deserves our sympathy. Fortunately it tends not to last for very long – and almost any diagnosis is likely to be a comfort after it!

What am I waiting for?

How much longer am I going to have to wait here like this, I wonder?
Sister said 'round about three o'clock'. Well, it's
Four now, and they haven't come yet.
I do wish they'd be quick:
They should be bringing the old lady back soon,
I should think. They took her down to the theatre soon after lunch.
– not that we had any lunch, of course, being down for
tests this afternoon –
I feel so stupid, lying here in this absurd flannel night shirt . . .
Oh, why don't they come!

Just listen to me, Lord, carrying on as usual
I can't think why I'm going on like this,
It isn't as if it was a serious operation.
It isn't as if I had anything to be frightened about.
Just routine tests – they must have done hundreds of them.
Thousands of them. (Oh why don't they come!)

He joked about it himself: said he'd 'never lost a patient from this one'
He was joking, of course.
So it's absolutely stupid for me to be frightened

And I'm not frightened, of course.
Not a bit.

But I wish they'd come.

Suggested reading:

Romans, Ch. 8. St Paul frequently has encouraging words for this kind of situation. In this chapter he reminds us that we have a source of protection and inner strength that we should never under-estimate: 'You are not controlled by the sinful nature but by the Spirit' (v. 4). This is another way of saying that we belong to Christ, and can call upon his strength in the hour of need. The references to 'the law' mean the rules we know we should keep in order to be good people. If we can't always keep them, we should remember that Christ has kept them for us, and not give up in despair. Trying to abide by rules we can't live up to can turn us against them – and them against us. So thank God for Christ! Paul is very conscious of his own human vulnerability, but he knows that because of what Christ has done, he, Paul, is secure: 'By him we cry Abba, Father' (v. 15).

13. Back to basics

Round the corner they come, at seven o'clock in the morning, trampling over one another, too interested in what they're talking about to look where they're going. A dozen conversations, each one loud and uninhibited and totally engrossing. These are the Domestics; you hear them before you see them. They are well named. In these impersonal surroundings these women somehow manage to be completely at home. Not only this, but they make the place seem like home to other people too, some of whom really appreciate it, being more home-sick than they ever believed it possible to be. Somehow the Hospital Domestics make things normal. *They*, at least, are not impressed by status. People are people to them – even people who've just walked across the bit of floor they've just scrubbed.

Emergency routine, tension, relaxation, the solemn and the farcical, in the middle of everything the Domestics go about their reassuring business of being themselves. This is why they are able to carry out their unofficial job, which is to be confidante and counsellor to patients. It's more natural to talk to the lady who is scrubbing your bed-space than the nurse who's giving you an injection. And, anyway, the nurses have so much to do, don't they? Domestics are so ordinary. For a lot of people this ordinariness is an important part of the cure.

Strategies

Sometimes I wonder why I took this job on.
God knows I've enough cleaning-up to do at home
I mean, with a family of four, and not to mention
Half of the neighbourhood kids in and out of the house all day
As well as giving my Dad a hand with his chores on Saturday
(Not that he makes much work, always neat as a pin
Having been in the Navy for twenty years)

41

Mind you, it's different here from home.
We do everything by numbers here. We're all lined up
In preparation for going on the wards; all lined up
With our electric floor-polishers and scrapers
And mops and buckets,
To carry out the strategic invasion of each ward on a Sunday morning.

And yet, for all our efficiency and discipline, it's just the same
Just the same job really
And we're the same people doing it, just the same
(Just a minute, love, I won't be a sec., just lift up your foot
While I do that bit of floor – that's right, dear, can you move your book,
I've got to wash the top of the locker, make it nice and clean)
And it's comforting for them, comforting for the patients
Something ordinary, ordinary people doing ordinary things
The things they do at home (Oh I say –
your hair looks nice, love, what do you use? That's funny,
That's what I do, too, but I can never get mine to look like that . . .)

Thank you, Lord, for ordinariness,
Ordinary things, ordinary jobs,
Ordinary people.
People like ourselves, Lord,
Who do not make us feel anxious.
Help us to use this ordinariness in your service.
As, reassured by the comforting and the familiar,
We gain confidence to venture into the unknown.

Suggested reading:

1 Corinthians, Ch. 3. Paul was very much aware of the ways in which people co-operate for one another's good. He was also very conscious that this is often ruined by the selfish attitudes that bring about rivalry. One says, 'I follow Paul', and another, 'I follow Apollos'. This kind of way of looking at life leads to the kind of rigid hierarchy in which the people who do really valuable work are overlooked because their jobs are not considered to be 'posh'. This is not God's way of assessing people, and 'the wisdom of this world

42

is foolishness in God's sight' (v. 19). For a wonderful picture of the world at work, read *Psalm 104*.

Part II

Some People

14. Coming home

The feeling of strangeness which you have when you first arrive in hospital is soon followed by another kind of feeling altogether. The ward is no longer strange. You live here now – for a few days or a few weeks, at any rate. You have managed to settle in and make yourself at home; after all, you're not alone – everybody here feels like you. But this discovery is made at some cost. The surer you begin to be of your new identity, your identity as a hospital patient, the member of a select brother- or sister-hood, the less secure you begin to feel in your own role, your accustomed family role as mother, father, husband, wife, son or daughter. After all, you are here and they are there; and there is so much distance between here and there that you might be in a different world.

Indeed, you are in a different world. It doesn't matter if the rest of your family are at the other end of the country or only a few hundred yards away, living just outside the hospital gates, they are separated from you by the emotional gulf dividing the initiated from the uninitiated. By coming into hospital, by settling down in hospital you have become, in a sense, 'another person'; lying in your hospital bed you survey your ordinary life from a point of vantage, as someone who is in a position to see things with a special clarity. You look critically at the situation you have temporarily left behind – your work, your friends, your family – yourself. Your new detachment makes some things stand out very clearly.

The things you notice now are the important things, the things that really matter. You become aware of the wood and the trees. People and places you have tended to take for granted are suddenly very dear to you indeed, and you reach back over the distance that divides you from them, and take them again to your heart. You are conscious of an experience of renewal, of having graduated, through suffering, to a greater awareness of the things that belong to your peace. This suffering, whether it is the pain involved in being ill, or the shock of having to leave everything familiar and come into the alien world of the hospital – or, as is usually the case, a mixture of both – is lived through in the presence of other people, in community with other men or women in the ward. The clarity it produces is clarity about relationship.

Neighbours

Excuse me, I'm sorry to be a nuisance,
But will you do something for me?
I'm just going down now, you see,
It's nothing much, shouldn't take long –
I've been waiting nearly three weeks – the machine broke down
And they had to send away for a part –
There's this lady called George, she's given up her turn for me.
I don't know
Her surname, but they call her George. She's got dark hair.
Please go and thank her, would you, it's so kind,
She's very worried about what's going to happen to her,
And she's got two young children.Thank you so much
Yes, she's a lovely person. It's funny you know,
I've been speaking to her for a fortnight now,
And I still don't know her real name.

Suggested reading:

Mark, Ch. 8: 22–24 – 'like trees walking around'. It certainly takes time to adjust to radical change, even when it's for the better. *Acts, Ch. 9: 1–19* shows how Paul, after his experience on the Damascus road, was left in a state of complete shock, as indicated by his blindness. He was soon given his sight back, at the hands of one of the new followers of Jesus, but he never saw things the same way again. . . . Extreme sorrow may have the same effect. In *Luke, Ch. 24*, the two disciples do not recognize Jesus, even though they have been talking to him for several hours. Their world was transformed when they realized who it was. For the effect that a chance meeting may have, see *John, Ch. 4: 1–30*. It was because Jesus was a stranger that the woman was able to talk to him; it was a completely unofficial occasion. Yet what he said to her moved her so much that her view of life was transformed: 'Could this be the Christ?'

15. Keep your distance!

Most of the patients sleep and eat in the wards. However, each ward has one or two single bedrooms, traditionally called 'side-wards'. You would think that most people would prefer to have one of these rooms rather than to share a ward with ten or even twenty other people: after all, it's not what most of us are used to, is it? It always takes a little time to get accustomed to performing intimate and embarrassing functions in close proximity to someone we don't know at all, and with a potential audience of eighteen other strangers. It's surprising though, how quickly such things cease to trouble us, as we learn that the space round our bed is *our* space and the person in the next bed is our friend. Once this happens we settle down quite quickly and start to appreciate the particular quality of camaraderie which comes from being 'on the same ward together', and which depends on the individuality of each person involved – in other words, on the very awkwardness and differences that caused so much trouble in the first place.

Unfortunately, those in the side rooms tend to miss out on this. As it turns out they weren't as lucky as they thought they were. Indeed, they can feel very lonely and neglected. What is worse, they tend to feel excluded. Which is why most men and women who have spent any length of time in hospital will tell you that they much prefer an open ward to a side room. It seems that it's better to have to adjust to too many folk than too few. You never adjust to too few.

Don't forget me . . .

Nine o'clock.
Visiting time's over. No one will come now
Too late.
My eyes ache. I can't read
Any more.

48

Only nine. Out there
They're still talking away. Last night,
They went on and on and on and on
Until half-past one. You'd think
They didn't need to sleep at all
Some people.
Perhaps they talk because they can't sleep,
Like me. Just like me. Only –
I've no one to talk to. I'll close my eyes
And pull the sheet over my ears
And pretend I'm talking to someone. Mary,
Doreen, Phyllis, Sue's bed is halfway down the ward –
Dear Sue. That was so kind, what she said this afternoon.
I'll think of her now
And I know she's thinking of me, as I am of her, and that's wonderful:
And I know she's thinking of me thinking of her
Which is even better.

Suggested reading:

Psalm 4. God is not punishing you by making you lonely; on the other hand he may be reminding you that he is always near you, to comfort you. The time before falling asleep is always hard to put up with when you are by yourself and away from home. You are always in his hands, wherever you are, and you don't know what good things he has in store. *Psalm 116* will remind you of how he has looked after you in the past, even when you were in the very gravest trouble. 'Here I am! I stand at the door and knock. If anyone hears my voice and opens the door, I will come in and eat with him and he with me' (*Revelation, Ch. 3: 20*).

16. Courage

The sparrow was rolling around on the ground, flapping its wings frantically. It was obviously in distress – 'What's the matter with it, poor little perisher?' 'Will it let you pick it up?' 'Hey, wait a minute, there's something wrong with its legs. Look, it's only got one leg.' 'Oh what a shame, what'll it do?' 'It's too late, it's dying.' But the sparrow wasn't dying, as a matter of fact. It was only having a dust bath. It pushed itself up with its one remaining leg and took off, flying up into the air. Nothing wrong with its wings, you see.

If you saw Elsie walk across the room, you'd be very worried about her. She walks slowly, on the outside edges of her feet, swaying about as though she's going to topple over and fall. Sometimes she does fall, and you have to help her up again. But we let her walk by herself because that's what she wants. Elsie had a stroke and couldn't walk at all for four years. A couple of weeks ago she was still having to be pushed in a chair. But there's nothing wrong with her courage. When Elsie sways and totters, Elsie flies.

Mrs Cross

Mrs Cross suffers in silence, never complaining –
She must be suffering, or she couldn't be so silent –
Could she?
And old Miss Birkett, how cheerful she is.
That cheerfulness, you know – .
It's really a sign of great courage.
You can always tell.
They don't say much, but inside . . .
Oh, how I wish I could be like that!
How I wish I had that kind of courage!
I haven't anything to complain about, really;
I knew this was going to hurt,
Nobody comes into hospital for fun do they?

I knew that when I came. But Lord, Lord –
I never thought it would hurt like this,
I really didn't –
I didn't think anything could hurt like this
You'd think they'd give you something to help,
Perhaps they would if I asked the nurse –
Only I don't like to ask;
I don't like being the only one to make a fuss.
After all, Mrs Cross and Miss Birkett must be going through much more
Much more than me
And there's really nothing much wrong with me
I wish I could be like them;
I wish I could be like them:
I *ought* to be like them . . .
Nurse, please nurse . . .
Nurse, do you think I . . . ?

Suggested reading:

Psalm 27 – 'The Lord is my light and my salvation – whom shall I
fear?' This is a verse to cling to. If you repeat it to yourself when
you are trying to rest, you'll find it a great comfort. It can also be
used as a kind of 'mantra' to relax your mind. Say it calmly over
and over again while you think about a favourite passage in the
Bible. If you go to sleep, it doesn't matter. The rest of the psalm is
very beautiful too, especially the quiet strength of the ending. Remember, 'oppressors' need not necessarily be other people; they
need not be people at all, but fears, powerful emotions, worrying
ideas – whatever it may be that is oppressing you. In *2 Corinthians,
Ch. 12: 1–10*, St Paul actually 'boasts' about the way his own weakness serves to reveal more clearly the strength of God. This is the
good purpose his very real failings serve; and it is the idea that
keeps him going when times are hard: 'for when I am weak, then I
am strong'.

17. A matter of life and death

People get very fond of each other in hospital. The urgency of the situation breaks barriers down, and deep friendships are often formed within the space of a few weeks. Besides it's not all that easy to 'keep yourself to yourself' in hospital, because everybody is physically so close to everybody else, and to remain aloof requires a positive effort at self-isolation; and even that breaks down after a bit. These ward friendships are quite genuine, and often last for years, long after patients have left hospital; the only abnormal thing about them is the short time which they take to develop – and also a certain quality of mutual honesty, the simple acceptance of each other without criticism, which always seems to mark them.

Both these things, speed of growth and quality of commitment, come from life in the presence of death. People are often unwilling to talk about death in hospital. But this doesn't mean that they are unaware of its presence. Indeed, it is because they are so conscious of it that they never talk about it. To talk about it seems 'unlucky'. Hospital patients cling together to gain assurance against the common enemy.

All of this means that when someone dies in a hospital ward, the survivors are bound to find out almost as soon as it happens. It's no good trying to hide the news from them in order to spare their feelings. They deserve to know, and they need to know. They deserve to receive truthful bulletins about the war in which they are all engaged; they need to feel that their contribution to the campaign is important enough for them to be treated with dignity, as adults, and not simply protected against 'unnecessary anxiety'.

In any case the grief people feel when somebody they care about dies can never be considered to be 'unnecessary'. It is a fact of life. It must somehow be lived through. But it does not always receive the recognition it deserves. Hospital staff frequently give the impression that they underestimate the depth and strength of the attachments formed between fellow patients on a ward by their refusal to 'come clean' about death so that the ward community may have a chance to support one another in the work of mourning. Sometimes they manage to give the impression that it is not the patients who are afraid of the idea of dying, but they themselves.

Who's fooling whom?

Lord, I've got a problem. That old Mrs Smith
I think I know why they've pulled the curtains round her bed;
She's dead, isn't she, Lord?
I'm not supposed to be awake yet
I'm not supposed to have seen it at all
I'll have to pretend I haven't seen it
Or the special trolley they use –
But the problem's not about me, Lord, not directly, anyway.
It's about Joan. Joan was specially fond of her, you see
She reminded her of her mother, who died last year
You see, Lord, Joan doesn't know what has happened, she's still asleep
But she'll wake up soon, any moment now;
Should I tell her, Lord?
You see, I don't really know, don't know officially, that is;
Should I just let her find out, just let her imagine the worst?
Please, excuse me a minute, Nurse . . . I just want to ask you –
It's about old Mrs Smith. Nurse –
Has she . . . ?

Lord, you have taught us that we should not be too afraid of dying –
That death is not the worst thing that can happen to us.
Help us to fight always to safeguard and preserve life
But as men and women who are not afraid of the truth.
The truth about life and death,
The truth about ourselves and other people,
So that the comfort we give may be real comfort,
Honest comfort.
Help us to acknowledge, every moment of our lives,
The things we cannot change.

Suggested reading:

1 Thessalonians, Ch. 4: 13–18. This may be difficult to take literally, particularly if you don't really believe in archangels. But there is no mistaking Paul's passionate commitment to his message that what happened to Jesus will also happen to those who call upon his name. As he rose, so will we; archangels are not the point! As for the impulse to pretend when somebody dies that nothing has happened, this does not seem to have been a problem in biblical times, as it is today. However, *Psalm 51* asks God for help in avoiding the impulse to 'cover things up', and in *Luke, Ch. 12: 1–2*, Jesus says: 'Be on your guard against the yeast of the Pharisees, which is hypocrisy. There is nothing concealed that will not be disclosed, or hidden that will not be made known.' He is not speaking about our attitude to death, of course – but the saying certainly seems relevant!

18. For valour

People are often very brave about being in hospital. They are even brave about having to have operations. I sometimes think they are too brave. A little too brave to be true. After all it's a frightening thing, the idea of somebody performing a surgical operation on your body. However skilful they may be, and surgeons are very skilful, it is your body that they are going to cut open – your body, you yourself. I think it would be very strange indeed if you didn't find that idea a bit frightening. Our bodies may sometimes seem more of a burden than a blessing, particularly when they aren't functioning properly and are causing us pain; but we're stuck with them all the same. We can't simply set them on one side because they don't work as well as we'd like them to – or better still send them away to be repaired! However skilful techniques may become, hospital can never really be exactly like repair-shops or factories, because it's we really, we ourselves, who are being repaired!

It seems to me that if we are determined to maintain that the idea of being operated on doesn't worry us at all, we're really trying to pretend that our bodies don't belong to us. But that isn't so: they do belong to us. In a very real sense, they are us. Body and personality are so closely knit together that whatever happens to the one is almost bound to some extent to affect the other. This seems particularly true about the effect the body has on the mind. If your body is going to receive some kind of violent shock, some assault upon its integrity, then your mind, your awareness of things and people is bound to become fearful. The body's mind is alarmed by the threat offered to the mind's body! The truth of the principle involved is most clearly seen in retrospect, in the powerful effect that even a small operation has upon the patient's whole nervous system and consequently upon his or her state of mind.

If this is so, and I really believe it is, then the patients who are facing operations have only one choice they can make. They can admit they are frightened, or they can pretend not to be. I think the first is harder to do than the second. Some people are very good at hiding fear, even from – especially from – themselves. But I don't believe it does them any good. For fear always has to be taken into account. And it is not entirely negative. It has its place in the scheme of things. It is a stage in the process of being cured which must be lived through. It is part of the truth about the situation. If it is denied, this can only happen at the cost of a general tautening and tightening of the whole personality, a refusal to open yourself to what is happening to you. And this may actually make your recovery a slower business than it need be.

To admit to yourself that, after all, you're scared, is a liberating experience. Liberating and relaxing. With the help of the Holy Spirit, in the skill of the surgeon and the courage which is the peculiar reward of honesty, you are able to go on from there.

Hospital corners

It's been a long shift, and he's very heavy
For such a little man
Little and old. Turn over John, don't
Make such a fuss. We're only making your bed.
It's my wife's birthday and she's dead.
Don't cry, John – we don't have tears
On this ward.

Heavens, she must have died years
Ago. Why is he *still* crying? Surely
He must have got over it!

There you are, John, your bed's made now
All you have to do is lie on it.
Don't think we don't understand, we all
Have our troubles, there's no need for tears.

Suggested reading:

Revelation, Ch. 7: 11–17 – 'and God will wipe away all tears from their eyes' (v. 17). Our final comfort comes from God and God alone. Even those who try to help us may draw back when the going is too heavy. Read *Matthew, Chs 26 and 27: 1–54*. It was not that the disciples rejected Jesus, but that they were unable to allow themselves to be fully involved in his suffering. It seems they found ways of avoiding knowing what was really going on. See also *Mark, Chs 14, 15; Luke, Chs 22, 23; John, Chs 18, 19.*

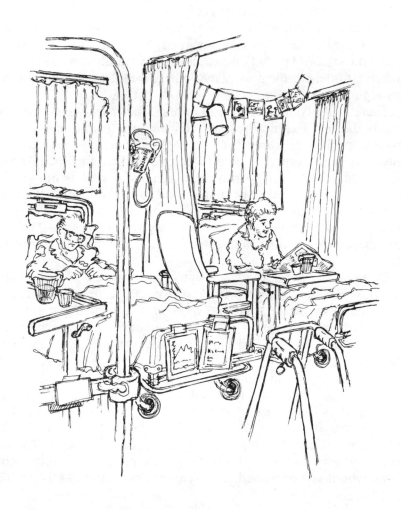

19. Neat and tidy

I realize that it's a strange thing to say, but there are some wards in some hospitals where you can't afford to be a patient – and I don't mean for financial reasons, either. Wards where you get the impression that the place is not really intended for sick people to be in at all. Untidy, messy, *sick* people get in the way in these wards. Pain is out of place in these wards; they are neat wards, tidy and 'well run', but it's hard to see what they are really for. Perhaps they exist to make the staff feel proud and successful; certainly it would be very difficult to defend them as places where people are helped to live through an illness.

There is always the danger, of course, that as ways of repairing our bodies get technically more efficient, the traditional ways of making people feel cared for as people and not as broken-down pieces of machinery, may tend to be overlooked. Sick people need the benefit of our insight into their feelings as well as our professional skill. They need to be understood as well as simply 'treated'. But in some wards you get the impression that the patients are too frightened to let anyone know what they really feel like. The pain and discomfort of their illness are increased by having to pretend that nothing is amiss.

On the other hand, there are signs that nowadays hospital staff are more aware of the need to take patients' feelings into account than they used to be; that the days of regimented patients and embattled staff are over. The days of embattled *patients*, however, are still with us, and perhaps they always will be. Embattled patients are those who are so determined to be courageous, so determined to proclaim their courage, that nobody else dare be a coward. And since coming into hospital makes most of us into cowards, this is as much as to say that nobody dare be honest. In some wards the atmosphere of socially imposed bravery is very noticeable indeed. It comes across as a kind of tension. There is usually at least one patient who will not – probably cannot – conform; who is too depressed, or too angry, or simply too ill, to hide his real feelings. It is *in comparison with him*, that the others are brave.

But, of course, they are not really brave at all. They are not brave enough to admit that they are just as anxious and unsure of their ability to cope as he is. They will not accept the truth about themselves. They are always 'perfectly all right, thank you'; they never have anything but praise for the hospital, and 'the wonderful work that you all do'. He, on the other hand, simply contents himself with saying that 'it's a good job there are such places'. He says it without much enthusiasm, and with obvious reservations; he is grateful, but, all the same . . .

Who are you kidding?

It's a good thing there are places like this.
There's something under this sheet, I can't get it flat
I don't see why I need a rubber sheet at all, I'm
Not incontinent, which reminds me
Nobody's been to change my catheter yet.
It's a good thing there are places like this.

Nurse, just a moment,
Please Nurse, d'you think you,
Nurse, Nurse, where are you?
Funny, there were nurses everywhere a minute ago
Now, when I need one, there's not a nurse in sight.
Excuse me, is there a nurse anywhere?
Excuse me . . .
It's a good job there are places like this.

Yes, that's right, I've had an operation
Yes, that's right, it *is* still rather sore
I was supposed to have had it done last week, but
It was put off you see
Twice. They're always very busy.
It's a good thing there are places like this.

What are you saying?

59

Sorry about that but it still hurts when I cough
And I seem to have caught a cold – What's that?
When I laugh? Well I'm sure it would
If I could. All the same, you know
It's a *very* good thing there are places like this.

Suggested reading:

Psalm 98 – 'Sing to the Lord a new song, for he has done marvellous things . . .' A song of triumphant thanksgiving for deliverance from whatever oppression has recently taken place. A song for coming into the light, leaving the darkness behind. A *new* song. Notice how wide-reaching it is, taking everything within its scope, 'all the ends of the earth'. See also *Psalm 100*, 'Shout for joy to the Lord, all the earth'. This psalm is only short, but it sums everything up for someone who wants to give thanks. (Perhaps it might even be learned off by heart. Try it if you find time hanging heavily!) *Psalm 103* contains the verse: 'He forgives all my sins and heals all my diseases' (v. 3). The glorious majesty of God reaches down to men and women in love. The very distance shows the wonderful nature of this love – that *he* should love *me!* Gratitude is the theme of *Luke, Ch. 17: 11–19* – 'Was none found to return and give praise to God except this foreigner?'

20. Role play

Look under the surface and you'll find a lot of vulnerable people work here. The face we usually see is the one turned to us; the fact that it changes out of all recognition when its owner looks away doesn't occur to us at all. If you don't know a person very well you're unlikely to spend much time thinking about his or her 'other faces'. The strange thing about hospitals, when you first arrive on the ward, is the number of people who don't seem to have any private existence at all. They only have a public face. Not the patients, who are surrounded by evidence of another life outside the hospital walls ranging from the small nephew's crayoned get-well card to the blessedly unsuitable diaphanous negligee. The staff, on the other hand, present a different aspect. These efficient, aloof men and women, who move so calmly and purposefully through the place performing their tasks with the quiet, unfussed skill which comes only after long practice. They are not quite real, and their unreality makes them frightening. What kind of people are they?

Well, of course, they're people like us. Like you and me. The 'calm efficiency' is a pose adopted for reasons of self-preservation. Intensive Care isn't the only place in the hospital where the staff wear masks! If you don't feel what you're supposed to feel, you can at least look as if you do. After all, most of the patients are trying very hard to look as if they felt happy and confident, and you don't have to be a patient to be vulnerable, do you?

On the other hand, a lot of these people aren't wearing masks that they have assumed for themselves, but ones that we have given them. Instead of allowing them to be themselves we have forced them to conform to an image we already had in our own minds, an idea of the hospital as an impersonal institution, a machine for mending bodies. No wonder they frighten us! But they don't really look like that at all. In fact, if you look a bit more closely you'll see a face very like your own.

Consultant

Outside this office there is a row of chairs
And a row of people sitting on them.
They are uncomfortable chairs, the kind with hard backs and seats –
Not like my chair in here –
Leather, padded, with arms.

I don't know how many people are sitting out there
On the other side of the wall; I didn't count them when I came in
I didn't even look at them.
In a minute, my secretary will show the first one in,
And then the second one – and so on until the morning is over.
Patient by patient
One by one
Each case scrupulously considered, clinically appraised.
But people taken out of context, out of their element. I keep quiet
But I can't hear them through this solid door –
They're probably not talking, anyway –
They are silent because of apprehension,
I, because I'm lonely.

Strange I didn't realize how lonely you could be
Sitting in a padded chair in a comfortable office . . .
I would rather be out there talking to the patients.
The patients I didn't look at when I came in;
I tell myself that I'm here to cure, not to comfort –
But sometimes I could do with a bit of comfort myself!
Help me, Lord, to choose the kind of success I really want
The kind of success you want me to have;
The kind of knowledge and understanding that will set me free,
So that I may give myself and not merely my skills,
The kind of courage that overcomes divisions and breaks through barriers,
So that I may stop and smile and talk, however shy I am or tired I feel –
For if I lose touch with others
I lose touch with you.

Suggested reading:

Romans, Ch. 12 is about fellowship and the understanding of other people's needs which is greatly increased by Christian belonging: 'For by the grace given me I say to every one of you: do not think of yourself more highly than you ought . . .' You will certainly need Christ's help in keeping Paul's high standards. At the same time we must remember how much Christ values us, how precious we are to him, to avoid valuing ourselves too lowly! If we learn to 'love one another' we can avoid both dangers, because our love, our valuing of one another will be *shared. John, Ch. 14* offers help to the lonely. 'In my Father's house' does not only refer to dying.

Part III

Living Here

21. Questions and answers

We shouldn't be surprised that hospitals tend to make people religious. Or rather, they bring out the innately religious element in everybody. I don't mean that everybody suddenly becomes very devout, so that they can accept what is happening to them without complaint, trusting God implicitly – although some people certainly have this experience – but almost everyone begins to question and to argue, 'Why has this happened?', 'What does it mean?' and 'Why has it happened to *me*?' This last is often kept rather quiet, because it seems a dodgy thing to be asking, the kind of question you don't really want answering. But it keeps cropping up, all the same. 'I keep arguing with God,' a young man said. 'I think he ought at least to give me a clue about what he has in mind.' He said it as if he were joking, but I knew he was deadly serious. He had broken his neck swimming too vigorously in a pool that was too small, and would never swim again. Or walk either. For Joan, a young housewife in a Regional Secure Unit, the question was rather different. She killed her husband and child while she was suffering from a mental illness, and now has to live the rest of her life with the knowledge of what she did. 'Why did God let me do this? Why did he let me do this to *them*?' Which is worse? – another useless question.

They are useless, pointless questions, yet we keep asking them; and if we don't actually put them into words – and some people are nervous about doing this, nervous about confronting God and demanding an answer because if you once take up that kind of attitude you never know what might happen – then we ask them implicitly by our puzzled restlessness, the extra anxiety and distress which we undergo in the presence of real calamities. We believe that if we could find an answer we would be able to make sense of what has happened; it wouldn't be explained away, of course, but it would at least be *explained*. This is a bit like applying a tourniquet to a fractured arm: it doesn't actually help the affected part. You can talk about the relationship between love and freedom in a sermon, but it doesn't make much sense on the ward. Not the right kind of sense, anyway. Much better to hold hands and shut up.

God doesn't shut up, however. He doesn't wait there in frustrated silence, wishing he could help, not knowing what to say. He doesn't search for words of healing and find only platitudes. I don't know what he says, but he says *something*. In his own way, and his own time, God says something uniquely different to everyone who questions him. A personal message. Not an *idea*, which someone else might have come up with, but an *experience*.

Listen to the trees

The wind sweeps round the corner of the hospital building, making the trees outside
Dip and sway.
I'm still lying here, looking at the trees,
Still asking the same question. The trees
Sway and bend,
Bow their backs, spring back again.
However hard it tries, the wind can't beat them
I lie here and watch, loving the trees –
They have life and joy and movement,
Everything I haven't got. You'd expect me
To hate them, I suppose. I did at first
But not now. They bear me up, the trees,
As if I'm being carried. With them
I ride out the storm.

Lord Christ, you come into our lives as a servant,
Putting things together for us,
Picking up our pieces,
Comforting our desperation.
You answer our questions in ways that work.
Beloved Handyman,
We would be nowhere without you.

66

Suggested reading:

Matthew, Ch. 11 – 'Are you the one who is to come, or are we to expect some other?' As unlikely a Messiah as Jesus was bound to be questioned. Not only John the Baptist's disciples, but Jesus's own wanted to know if there was any point in pinning their hopes on him (*Mark, Ch. 10: 28–30; Matthew, Ch. 19: 27–29*). Jesus describes how people's fixed ideas about life have blinded them to the truth about God, whether it be revealed in scripture, the message of John the Baptist, or his own mission and ministry. There is a time when argument has to stop – a time for throwing yourself on God's mercy and re-discovering his love. The chapter (*Matthew 11*) is treasured by all who read the New Testament for the way it ends: 'Come to me, all whose work is hard, whose load is heavy; and I will give you relief' (v. 28).

22. People and machines

Human compassion, human insight, human skill, the ability to weigh up situations and make decisions. These are the most important things involved in the way the hospital works. But they are not the only things. Modern hospitals are full of expensive and sophisticated machinery. As time goes on, it becomes more expensive and more sophisticated, more able to deal with the problems of diagnosis and therapy which occur every day in every hospital in the world. New machines are invented or evolve, and existing ones are perfected or made more reliable. The public is kept informed of every technical advance, every scientific breakthrough, so that we might be forgiven for thinking that very soon there will be a machine for curing everything. We get the impression that we are living on the eve of a Utopian age of medicine, when there will simply be no more heights to scale, no more problems to solve. It will all be done by machines.

It only takes a moment's reflection to realize that this is, and can only be, a fantasy. For even the most superb techniques and the most advanced machines need people to work them: to choose when and if to set them going. Apart from which, there are so many things that, if they are to be done properly, must be done *personally*. For example, machines can't comfort the distressed in any deep or lasting way. They are no good at working through emotional problems. Tablets and injections may be marvellous at relieving anxiety, but they can't give you somebody to depend on, someone who understands and encourages. What kind of machine could express silent sympathy? It could perhaps perform the function of your damaged kidney admirably; but it wouldn't be much good at holding your hand.

There is one advantage in machines, however. And it's a great advantage. They don't get tired. Hospitals run on people, and people get very tired indeed. People who work in hospitals get so exhausted from time to time that they can even fall asleep while they are working. Nurses on night duty, consultants with huge case-loads, housemen on call for several days at a stretch. The staff shortage makes the situation more extreme, because available personnel have to work longer hours. But the 'myth of the machine' continues to grow and flourish, distracting attention from the great need for more people, more ordinary human beings – limited, often tired out, but still capable of sympathy and insight.

Still life

I went to see Elizabeth on Intensive Care.
She looked very beautiful, very serene, like a statue carved in living tissue,
An angel in a trance.

O Lord, give her back to us, she's not an angel,
She's an ordinary human being –
Although I can see now how beautiful,
How very beautiful. I put out my hand to touch her
It's hard because of all the wires and attachments
Where the hospital is holding her to itself
So I can hardly lay a finger on her anywhere.
Touch her yourself, Lord, I can't –

Touch Elizabeth. No ifs or buts,
Let your healing power give life to her mortal body,
Restore her senses and renew her mind, to love more deeply and love more truly
Than ever before. Do it, Lord,
Do this amazing thing. As you raised your Son from the grave,
Raise Elizabeth now from this living death
And give her to herself and to us.

Suggested reading:

John, Ch. 11: 1–44. A story of human grief and hope, which also turns out to be about the power of God in Christ and the triumph

69

of love. Notice how Jesus reveals his true identity to Martha, and is recognized by her, before he actually brings Lazarus back to life – as he said to Thomas, 'blessed are those who have not seen, and yet have believed' (Ch. 20, v. 29). With regard to our modern dependence on technology, read *James, 5: 13–16*. When all is said and done, healing is what takes place among people – although there is nothing at all to stop them being technicians!

23. Chaplain

I must admit – and I say it with some shame – that I thought the job of being a hospital chaplain would be easier than this. Easier than reading books and passing examinations. Easier than preaching sermons. Because you don't have to do anything. You simply have to sit and listen. Listen with all your attention – ears, mind, and heart. And try not to say anything.

That's the difficult part, however. The job here, the thing that's got to be mastered, is *not saying anything*. Difficult for people like parsons, who tend to talk a lot to fill in the gaps. The gaps make us anxious. 'Oh, it's all right for so-and-so, he can always find something to say.' Yes, I'm sure he can. But can he always find confidence to stop? To *shut up*? A lot of clergy tend to have this problem. You see, it goes with the job, in a way. It's not just that a lot of us are anxious and nervy – OK, call it sensitive, if you like – it's that we're professionals. Like doctors and nurses (and plumbers and traffic wardens and men who lay carpets), we're specially trained to change situations. To make things work. The way we do this is by 'providing the answer'. The advice, the explanation, the word of comfort. The *theological* answer. This is what we're trained to do, and it's what we do. On every possible occasion. We can't just listen and accept. We must somehow use our skills to deal with what's happening. We have our ointments and our plasters. We must apply them. That's what we're *for*.

At least, it's what we seem to think we're for. A lot of the people who speak to us think we're here for something rather different. They think we're here to listen to them. That's what they want us to do. Listen to them and understand them. Understand and *accept* them. At least accept the fact that they're feeling and thinking in a certain way, and that that is their message to us. This is the way I am. Do you understand me?

And what do we do? I'll tell you what I do, anyway. I barge in with an answer I happen to have ready about my person. It's not *the* answer of course, but it seems to fit the case of someone more or less like them, someone with a problem more or less like theirs, someone I once met, someone I read about in a book. Someone like *me*, perhaps. An answer about my person.

The other day I was called into one of the hospitals where I'm the Chaplain, at about half-past eight in the morning. It was a Bank Holiday, and I was intending to go in a bit later that day. It was the Accident Unit, and they said I was to hurry along as quickly as I could. There had been a cot death. Would I go along and say some prayers and comfort the young mother? And so I got up and went, not really knowing what to expect . . .

'She's in there, waiting for you.' There is the girl, sitting facing the cot with the dead child in it. There's a nurse standing behind her chair with one hand on her shoulder. 'Is it a . . . is *he* a boy, or a girl?' It turns out she was a little girl. The mother says nothing. She doesn't look at me, but continues to stare ahead at the wall, not saying anything. I say, 'I've come to bless her for you. We thought you might like that.' At this piece of inanity the mother looks straight at me. 'That's how I found her when I woke up. I looked in the cot and that's how she was.' She sounds defensive. Immediately I begin to wonder. I can't help it. To stop myself being suspicious, I go over to the mother and put my hand on her other shoulder, and say, 'Tell me her name.' 'Susan.' At the cot: 'Susan, I bless you in the name of the Father, the Son, and the Holy Spirit.' That's what I say, because I can't think of anything else to say. I'd like to baptise the child, but I can't because she's dead. Then I say, 'Lord, accept this spiritual baptism. We commend Susan to you in the name of Christ.' Then I add, on an impulse, 'And bless . . . what's your name, love?' 'Christine.' 'And bless Christine, too.' Christine is still staring at the wall. She hasn't looked at me again. The nurse puts her arm further round her shoulders, giving her a cuddle. I'm full of admiration for this nurse. I wonder if she knows more than I do. Does she feel suspicious too? I tell myself I shouldn't feel that way, these things happen. I tell myself, say something. Say something to make things better for her. To make things easier for me. Time stretches on, my muscles begin to stretch in my legs and arms and I begin to feel desperate. I tell myself that I ought to get out. I've done my job, such as it was, and if I can't be of any help I ought to get out. I say, 'Well Christine, at least we gave her a blessing. Now she's quite safe.' Christine doesn't react, and I begin to think about what I just said – 'at least' – 'now she's quite safe'. Better to have said nothing at all! But I can't say nothing! I have to try. Oh Lord, tell me what to say. Don't keep me hanging on here, not helping, probably making things worse. Tell me something I could say. Time stretches out. Still nothing is said. I can't move now, I'm rooted to the spot. I know I must stay, even though I feel I'm no help at all. And the thought comes very clear and distinct. 'This is it. This is what it's all about.'

I'm not at all sure what the thought means; but I wait a bit longer. Then, at last, I'm able to turn to go out. Instead I go over to Christine and take her hand. 'It's just that we don't think you should feel guilty. We just want to make sure you don't feel it's your fault, don't we nurse?' The nurse says, very definitely, 'No, we don't.' Christine looks up at her and smiles.

Lord, if there're things we can't say that should be said,
Help us to let you say them for us.
Otherwise, help us to be silent.

Suggested reading:

1 Corinthians, Ch. 15: 50–58. The Christian hope is triumphantly expressed. Paul's certainty may be hard to come to terms with if you read this immediately after the kind of tragic happening described here. He was a man of tremendous faith, and it is really his faith that helps us here – he was as certain as this, and we are reassured and strengthened by his testimony, which undergirds our own trust in God. As far as comforting those immediately involved goes, a look or a touch of the hand may speak volumes. If words are called for, remember Jesus's instructions to his disciples: 'What you are to say will be given you when the time comes' (*Matthew, Ch. 10: 19*). I myself find great comfort in *John, Ch. 20*, particularly the story of Mary Magdalen and the 'gardener' – the single totally unexpected word transforming her world – but all the Resurrection stories have tremendous power when we take them personally and apply them to our own lives. Rabboni ... (See also *John, Ch. 11: 17–35* – Jesus wept.)

24. The chapel

At the heart of the hospital is the chapel. Its services are a kind of commentary on all the helping and loving and sharing that lie at the very heart of the hospital. This is why they never seem out of place, even in this scientific world of clinical expertise. Ward Communion is a good example. This strange, confident, little service which suddenly irrupts into the privacy of their shared bedroom, is about them and for them – whatever their own personal views may be about the church and religion. Because it is about *caring* and about *sharing*.

I confess that there's something here that I can't really put into words. Something happens to differences between one religion and another, or even between any religion and no religion at all. It's to do with discovering that, deep down, at the very basic level, you don't belong to yourself but to one another; and that the truth you're searching for is actually the truth of belonging. This isn't, in itself, any specific religion, it's the ground in which particular religions grow, and it unites all our religions at their most basic level, the level of our shared humanity. This bed, this ward, is a focus of the whole hospital; this patient is all patients. This, I say, is something that the ward itself knows, and appreciates, and seems to accept. Which is why even the least 'religious' person there will put up with the invasion of his or her precariously held privacy; and why, as the service proceeds, more and more people join in, if they happen to know the prayers, or close their eyes and smile, if they don't.

And so, for a few minutes, the ward does, in fact, become a kind of church, as the sacramental presence of Christ draws towards itself all the loving and hoping, all the sharing, and trusting, all the self-giving, all the service, that lives in this place, and 'Christ's healing gifts abound' here, in the hospital ward, in the experience of every one of us.

This is the hospital chapel. Shhh . . .
It's very quiet and peaceful in here.
Dedicated to the patients and staff of the hospital by the millowners and miners who paid for it,
Dedicated on such and such a day, month and year —
Dedicated to the blessed relief of pain, to healing and compassion and service
Dedicated to dedication —
To be a place of peacefulness and quietness,
Where people can sit for a few moments after the strain of visiting a loved member of the family.
And for patients to come to on a Sunday morning for the service.

It's very quiet and peaceful in here, so that if there's a moment to spare,
A nurse or even a doctor, seeking refuge in tranquillity,
May make an unofficial entrance, unofficial or semi-official.
The little light burns in front of the curtains where the bread and wine
Are kept quietly, quietly bringing them to our attention.
When the service begins the altar candles are lit,
But in the meantime now, when the chapel is empty,
The sanctuary light flickers in the quietness of the chapel,
The chapel-light burns quietly in the theatres and wards of the hospital.

Forgive us, Lord —
Though we work in the place where you are still working
Among the people whom you love, and with whom you have made your home,
We need this opportunity of recognizing you in silence and in symbol
For all the times we encounter you in other places
And pass you by without acknowledgement.

Suggested reading:

John, Ch. 2: 13–22. John describes Jesus's powerful reaction to the profaning of the Jerusalem temple (see also *Matthew, Ch. 21: 12–13; Mark, Ch. 11: 15–17; Luke, Ch. 19: 45–46*). Jesus pays the building the honour due to it as the House of God. The new temple, however, is to be different. It is to be one 'not made with human hands'. The living way to worship God is through the faith which makes us members of Christ's body. So you don't need to be able to get to the hospital chapel to reach him! Even so, the worship of the temple is precious to Christians because the psalms we use in our own services came from this source and reflect feelings that are timeless. Read *Psalm 43. Luke, Ch. 2*, after telling about Jesus's birth, describes two incidents during his early years when he visited the temple, for his Presentation and for the yearly Feast of the Passover. Notice that Jesus, the Son of God, goes to the temple to learn about his Father. This concern for the temple comes to the fore again at the time of his entry into Jerusalem before the Crucifixion (*Luke, Ch. 19: 45–46*). From now on, until the day of the Last Supper, he would be teaching 'at the temple' (*Luke, Chs 20, 21*). In *Luke, Ch. 4: 14–30*, at the beginning of his ministry, he taught in the synagogues of Galilee, including his own local one at Nazareth, where he reminded the congregation of a few 'home truths'.

25. Godspeed

You always seem to be saying goodbye now. When you first came in, to the people you love and had to leave behind; again and again when they came to visit you, and no sooner arrived than had to be off again, off back to the old places and tasks, to the life you loved, leaving you here behind them; and now to these people in the hospital ward, whom you have, in some strange way, in so short a time, come to love too.

In some strange way and in so short a time. You don't need to be in a ward very long before you start feeling more and more that you belong there. People who spend long periods of time in hospital report that the first three weeks are the worse; by which they mean that at the end of that time they are usually properly 'settled in' so that although, of course, they would much rather be fit and at home with their families, they no longer feel quite so strange and uncomfortable – so out of place. Once having reached this stage, they can face the idea of staying in hospital until they are really well again, even though this may take a long time – longer than they had hoped when they first came into the ward, three weeks ago.

This may seem a little surprising. After all, three weeks is not really very long – although in hospital it tends to feel more like three months! How is it, then, that patients manage to come to terms with their new situation so rapidly? Hospital is a completely new world, totally different from the world they have been used to outside. How do they come to adapt so well to it?

Hospital life is a strange mixture of boredom and intensity. Although there are long intervals in which nothing very much seems to happen, the emotional pitch of life is heightened by the constant awareness of danger; danger to others if not directly to ourselves – and always, therefore, to ourselves *by implication*. In matters which concern sickness and health, ordinary decisions take on a special significance. Life is lived with a peculiar intensity, as it sometimes is during a war, when people become alert to the possibility of dying; death not as a hypothesis, but as a real presence in the immediate situation. What happens in fact is that awareness of death in this way makes life more precious than ever, so that the things that belong to being alive, *to knowing that one is alive* – notably the relationships with other people that affect the particular quality of our life, its special humanity – are sought after and enjoyed with greater determination. In the presence of death, life is somehow 'speeded up'. In the crisis of this intense experience of reality – of the things that really matter, and of *how much* they really matter – it is deepened and enriched.

Which is why, of course, we grow so fond of one another in so short a time. And why we are so sad when our friends leave hospital before us, even though we may only have known them for a few weeks or days. It is also the reason why, when the time comes, we are so reluctant to leave ourselves. We haven't done much while we have been in hospital. In fact, we've hardly done anything at all. But during those long hours of boredom and discomfort, during all the waiting around and trying to kill time, we have actually been living life in a way that we have rarely had an opportunity to do before: experiencing it double-strength, double-speed. This is the kind of thing that people don't forget. Psychologists call it a 'learning experience' – which is another way of saying that, as time goes on, we begin to understand it better and appreciate it more, and to measure our 'normal' way of living with the way things were then, when ordinary people and events seemed to matter so much. When life was so valuable, all of a sudden.

Which is why so many ex-patients look back on their time in hospital and say: 'I would not have missed this. Despite the anxiety and discomfort and boredom – despite the pain – I would not have missed it.'

At night

At night the great building closes in on itself.
During these long hours the hospital seems to be protecting something
Contracting in and yet expanding outwards
The corridors longer, warmer, darker,
Nothing public anymore, except the main staircase

79

Which is ablaze with light and totally deserted.
At the top of the stairs, silhouetted against the darkness
One of the domestics has left a mop and bucket.
Along the dimly lit corridor two nurses come
Giggling and hushing each other.

Here in the ward, out of sight of Sister's station
There's a kind of concentrated dimness. The beds
Are breathing heavily like strange problematical animals.
The atmosphere is part laboratory, part barrack-room,
Part nursery. It's the nursery that dominates, a sense
Of something rare and precious, something unspoken,
To be protected. The hospital sleeps and watches
Hugging its purpose to itself.

Suggested reading:

Psalms 23, 147 – 'The Lord . . . heals the broken-hearted and binds up their wounds.' In some ways this is 'the valley of the shadow', even though it is a place of healing. Perhaps, in a way, the two things are the same. Certainly, people are more conscious of the fact of death when they come into hospital than they usually are – even when it is only for the removal of a toe nail. At the same time, it is surprising how few of us actually thank hospitals, or even doctors and nurses. And then, it's very often the least likely ones. (See *Luke, Ch. 17: 11–19.*)

'And surely I will be with you always, to the very end of the age' (Matthew, Ch. 28: v. 20).